# Say It With Music

## 11 Irving Berlin Songs

*Piano Solo Arrangements by*

### Geoff Haydon & Jim Lyke

*Edited by*

### Robert Pace

Tracks 1, 2, 3

# Alexander's Ragtime Band

words and music by Irving Berlin
arranged by Geoff Haydon and Jim Lyke

# A Pretty Girl Is Like A Melody

Tracks 4, 5, 6

words and music by Irving Berlin
arranged by Geoff Haydon and Jim Lyke

start up-on a mar-a-thon And run a-round your brain you can't es-

cape _____ she's in your mem-o-ry, _____ By

morn - ing, night and noon _____

leave you and then come back a - gain A

pret - ty girl is just like a pret - ty tune _____

# When The Midnight Choo-Choo
# Leaves For Alabam'

words and music by Irving Berlin
arranged by Geoff Haydon and Jim Lyke

2429

# Say It With Music

words and music by Irving Berlin
arranged by Geoff Haydon and Jim Lyke

to the strains of Cho-pin or Liszt. *mf* A

mel - - - o - dy mel - - - low

played on a cel - - - lo

helps mis - ter cu - pid a - long, *f* So

say it with a beau - ti - ful song. *mp*

# Play A Simple Melody

words and music by Irving Berlin
arranged by Geoff Haydon and Jim Lyke

# That International Rag

Tracks 16, 17, 18

words and music by Irving Berlin
arranged by Geoff Haydon and Jim Lyke

14

# All By Myself

words and music by Irving Berlin
arranged by Geoff Haydon and Jim Lyke

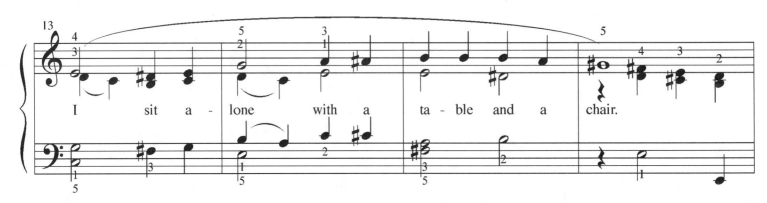

So un-hap-py there, play-ing sol-i-taire. *rit.* - - - -

All by my-self I get lone-ly,___ watch-ing the clock on the shelf.___ I'd love to rest my wear-y head on some-bod-y's should-er.___ I hate___ to grow old-er all by my-self. *rit.* - - - -

# The Road That Leads To Love

words and music by Irving Berlin
arranged by Geoff Haydon and Jim Lyke

Moderately slow ♩ = 90

seldom is all that it seems. To
have, to hold, to love and car - ess, is
all we can ask from a - bove. For the
road that leads to hap - pi - ness, is the
road that leads to love.

Tracks 25, 26, 27

# You'd Be Surprised

words and music by Irving Berlin
arranged by Geoff Haydon and Jim Lyke

He's got the face of an An - gel but, there's a dev-il in his eye.___ He's such a

del-i-cate thing but when he starts in to squeeze,___ you'd be sur - prised. He does-n't

look ve-ry strong but when you sit on his knees,___ you'd be sur - prised.___

At a part___y or at a ball,___ I've got to ad-mit___ he's noth-ing at all,___ but in an

ea - sy chair,___ you'd be suur - prised.___

2429

Tracks 28, 29, 30

# Everybody Step

words and music by Irving Berlin
arranged by Geoff Haydon and Jim Lyke

Ev-'ry-bod-y step to the syn-co-pa-ted rhy-thm, Let's be go-in' with them when they be-gin.

You'll be say-in' yes sir, the band is grand. He's the best prof-ess-or in all the land.

Lis-ten to the pep that-e - merg-es from the mid-dle of the jaz-zy fid-dle un-der his chin.

# I Love A Piano

Tracks 31, 32, 33

words and music by Irving Berlin
arranged by Geoff Haydon and Jim Lyke

I love to run my fin-gers o'er the keys___ the i - vor-ies and with the

ped-al___ I love to med-dle___ not on-ly mu - sic from Broad - way.___ I'm so de-

light-ed___ if I'm in - vi - ted___ to hear a long hair gen-ius play. So you can

keep your fid-dle and your bow.___ Give me a P - I - A - N - O, oh, oh, I love to

stop right___ be-side an up-right, or a high toned ba-by grand.

# THE GOLDEN ERA OF AMERICAN POPULAR SONG

Irving Berlin, the composer in this collection of Tin Pan Alley, show, and movie tunes, wrote in an era that became known as the Golden Age of American Popular Song. This period began roughly in the 1920's and lasted until the advent of rock music in the 1960's. Berlin wrote mostly for Broadway musicals and revues, but his songs can also be found in Hollywood musicals. Many of his songs became "standards" and were usually written in a 32 bar format. They have become favorites of many jazz musicians who improvise on the harmonic scheme of the tune. Berlin's music and lyrics were popular with singers such as Frank Sinatra, Ella Fitzgerald, Harry Connick, Jr., Tony Bennett, and others. When performing the songs in this album, study the lyrics. The lyrics will help you shape the phrases and build an effective interpretation.

# IRVING BERLIN

Irving Berlin (1888-1989) grew up in poverty, on the lower east side of New York. He began his musical career as a singing waiter, and taught himself to play the piano. His first "hit" song was **Alexander's Ragtime Band.** It sold over a million copies. He founded his own publishing company and later built (with his partner Sam Harris) the Music Box Theatre on Broadway. In this theatre, which still presents shows today, he produced many revues featuring his own songs. These were known as the Music Box Revues. Berlin also composed many songs for Hollywood musicals featuring the great dancer Fred Astaire. Berlin's most famous Broadway musical was *Annie Get Your Gun.* It was in this show that the anthem for all show business people, **There's No Business Like Show Business,** was introduced. Other Berlin songs include **God Bless America, White Christmas,** and **Blue Skies.** Berlin lived to be 101 years old.